T0156514

3 Steps To Recharge YOU!

A Simple Guide to Eliminate the Burnout
&
Rekindle the Passion Within

De Vida Bell, LCSW

iUniverse, Inc.
New York   Bloomington

3 Steps To Recharge YOU!
A Simple Guide to Eliminate the Burnout & Rekindle the Passion Within

You may direct your friends, colleagues, and associates to their own personal copy at:

http://www.mahoganyvida.com/3stepstorechargeyou.com.

Published by

Mahogany Vida Enterprises, LLC
4654 East Ave. S, Suite 195
Palmdale CA 93552
1-661-349-7565
www.mahoganyvida.com

iUniverse books may be ordered through booksellers or by contacting:

iUniverse
1663 Liberty Drive
Bloomington, IN 47403
www.iuniverse.com
1-800-Authors (1-800-288-4677)

ISBN: 978-1-4502-0473-6 (pbk)
ISBN: 978-1-4502-0474-3 (ebook)

Printed in the United States of America

iUniverse rev. date: 1/18/10

3 Steps To Recharge YOU is dedicated to my family and friends who have supported and guided me, and to those who constantly juggle "busy" schedules and "active" lifestyles en route to a life filled with happiness, accomplishment and purpose.

CONTENTS

Introductions & Acknowledgements

"Appreciate your uniqueness. Never in history has there been anyone exactly like you. Being one of a kind, you must be the best YOU, you can possibly be; develop your talents to the fullest. You can do anything you wish to do; the only limitation is your will. Make the most of the one and only you." - Bob Keeshan

As a Licensed Clinical Social Worker, entrepreneur, mentor, advocate, mother and wife, I realized that in life you must pick your battles. The struggles that life brings are not limited to one particular socioeconomic group, race, age, religion or geographic location. No, I firmly believe that in life, "struggle" is what I would definitely categorize as an equal opportunity employer. Everyone has the same opportunity to be affected by an issue or situation. How you or I may be affected is really dependent on how we, as individuals, choose to define it. We ultimately have two choices. We can define it as an issue or problem or we can reformat it and categorize it as a minor obstacle or challenge.

An issue or problem breeds negativity and helplessness and leaves little room for soluble solutions and positive movement.

An obstacle or challenge offers opportunities for self discovery, growth and/or development.

Think about the last obstacle you encountered. How did you embrace it – as a problem or a challenge? How did it affect you – positive or negative? And, what did you learn from it? Defining how you choose to embrace a situation will not only have an effect on your attitude and behavior but will ultimately influence the overall outcome as well.

As you read through *3 Steps To Recharge YOU*, I encourage you to use it as a Guide; A companion to assist in analyzing and understanding your thoughts, emotions, and decisions. If you're ready to improve the quality of your life and are serious about making a change and taking action than this Guide is for you. This book will take you on a personal journey of self-discovery only if you are willing to make a commitment and allow yourself to be open to new concepts and ideas. Before we begin, I have two opportunities for you.

The first opportunity is for you to read this Book in its entirety while being open and honest with yourself.

This information is ultimately for you and will assist you in soaring to new heights of self awareness. Sometimes, in order for you to move forward you need to reflect on the past, live in the present, and plan for the future. I've provided a **Summary of Reflections** at the end of each chapter to assist you in analyzing the information you just read. In addition, I've incorporated a personal note section to jot down thoughts, words and/or ideas you may have, from each reflection. Utilize your notations as a customized bookmark and as a reminder of concepts and actions during future chapter reviews. Also, you may use this section as an energy booster and tool for self-discovery and interpretation. It all starts with getting back to basics, ground zero. Getting back to the basics of who you are, is the foundation from which your thoughts, beliefs and experiences began. Anytime is the right time to bounce back and rekindle the inner you.

The majority of us, by process of elimination, are juggling busy schedules, wearing multiple hats, fulfilling a multitude of responsibilities and are our own worst enemies and/or critics. And, because of that, we put more undue strain on ourselves than others put on us, loosing a sense of personal self. As you rediscover the hidden you, use this YOU time to embrace the wonders YOU have to offer. Sometimes all it takes is a little shifting in our own personal climate and mindset to rekindle the strength that resides within all of us.

The second opportunity is for you to complete the **Action Item Boot Camp** at the end of each chapter. I recommend using one of the following two options to record your answers to each exercise:

- This Book
- Mahogany Vida Journal

Taking action through brainstorming, identification and discovery brings awareness and insight into the forefront of WHO you are as a person. Once you complete the Boot Camp Exercises, I encourage you to continue using them as an aide to increase your energy and self esteem and reduce stress and fatigue.

As you embark on this journey, your goal is to eliminate the burnout and rekindle the passion within. Use the tools on the following pages to refine, custom craft and redevelop the person you desire to be. I have used these tools in developing the three steps not only in my own personal and professional life but have also taught them to people of all ages struggling to overcome life's challenges.

You are welcome to visit my other websites and communities:

- The Official Site of Mahogany Vida Enterprises
  – https://mahoganyvida.com,

- Mahogany Vida's Community Connection
  – http://blog.mahoganyvida.com,

- Facebook Fan Page
  – http://www.facebook.com/devidafanpage,

- Twitter
  – www.twitter.com/devidabell.

Feel free to contact me with any questions and feedback. I look forward to hearing about your journey toward success.

My email address is devida@mahoganyvida.com.

Love and Success,

De Vida

CHAPTER 1

Analysis

"There are two primary choices in life: to accept conditions as they exist, or accept the responsibility for changing them."
– Denis Waitley

In life we have all made mistakes for whatever reason, I know I have, but that's null and void at this moment. What is important, however, is that we look at our present situation and analyze it. Ask yourself, what's going on that's "positive" in my life – personally and/ or professionally? When thinking about this question, concentrate only on the positive things.

I know it may be difficult to not slide in some "negative" thoughts as you answer these questions but it's important that you begin to make a conscious effort to shift your mindset towards optimism if you're going to move toward living life on your terms. It's easy to concentrate on what's going "wrong" or "what's not working." Why, because negativity surrounds our daily lives whether we're at home, work, school or in the community. We hear it, breathe it and see it whether we're talking on the telephone, watching television or listening to music or the radio. It is because of this negativity that we need to consciously make the effort towards that mind shift switch.

By default, society continues to show us the negativity of the world and by not engaging in the process for change we are unconsciously buying into the notion that so unmistakably creeps into our pores without our permission. So, in order to eliminate that unkindly flow of poisonous fumes, we need to do whatever it takes to restore a sense of belonging and control within ourselves, our mind, and the lives that we lead daily.

We start this by making a list of dreams and defining, in detail, what we would like to achieve as of today because it is only at this particular moment that we have a sense of belonging. My oldest daughter once told me that for every second that passes a moment has gone and cannot be repeated exactly yet can be made to replicate it. The wind may blow in a different direction, a different car may pass by, or your heart may skip that one extra beat and the moment is gone. All you have in this precious lifetime is the current moment in time with your thoughts, emotions and memories.

So often when I ask people to define their dreams they look at me with a puzzled look on their faces as though I were speaking a foreign language. Why, because to ask someone whose life is filled with death, destruction, turmoil or who has lost a sense of being or control has forgotten what it was like to dream. Many times the blame is placed on our "chaotic" lifestyle as the reason we don't have time to live, dream, let alone think. One can have a challenging lifestyle without labeling it as chaotic if they know how to balance the areas in their life. Also, by labeling it as "chaotic," you release negative energy. As we get older we forget to dream about the possibilities life has to offer, believing that there is a no way our dreams can come true based on our past or current situations.

The word *"anxiety"* fits right in the scheme of things; worrying what others would say and think if they were to dream aloud fearing to be judged or ridiculed. This word also encompasses fears of the unknown, concern over situations beyond our control, and apprehension about the future. When anxiety kicks in, people forget about the journey because they are overly consumed with the end result which generally is not as important as the process. When you think about something you want to achieve, customarily you look at the end result but if you don't also pay attention to the process, how can you duplicate it should the opportunity present itself. You need to be able to reflect not only on the success but also understand the system you put into place to replicate the same desired results the next time around.

Here's an example.

Take two people - one was given a million dollars and the other had worked all of his/her life to receive the same amount of money. Which one do you think would "traditionally" not only appreciate the money more but would also take extra measures to ensure its longevity and increased interest? If you took a survey of people from various socioeconomic groups, genders, ages, cultures and backgrounds, you're guaranteed to get different results.

The person who was given the million would tend to be a thriftier spender, purchasing items on a whim without regards to cost. Although they may have previously been conservative in their spending techniques, given this new opportunity, their tide has changed for the moment giving sparingly to others as well as themselves.

The person who worked for the million, on the other hand, would continue to be frugal with their finances, cautiously watching every dime and putting percentages away via investments, separate accounts and other diverse methods to instill a safety net for the future. Although they may spend more liberally, then in the past, their financial boundaries continue to be set daily, reviewing, recording, and tracking each penny spent whether personally or by an entrusted financial advisor.

The point is, life cannot necessarily easily be predicted but it can be controlled. All you have is today because tomorrow is undetermined no matter how much you plan – nature will take its course. No need to worry what others think and say because in the end it is your thoughts and choices that will determine your outcome. The *3 Steps to Recharge YOU Seminar*, provides an interactive training on how to create your personal dreams list, eliminating outside influences while refocusing on dreams from childhood and beyond.

As adults, we tend to limit our dreams based on others thoughts, comments and/or ideas of who *they* think we are or should become. We narrow our vision based on others words diminishing our own expectations. We pay attention to circumstantial evidence and advice given by those outside of our support network which results in our talking ourselves out of jobs, relationships, activities, and things we may be interested in doing, learning and experiencing. We tell ourselves we can't accomplish a once ignited dream due to past disappointments or circumstances. These thoughts lower our belief system. The alternative… advocating for ourselves and renaming the word "problem" to "challenge," for a new and improved future while refusing to be stigmatized or labialized by the events of our past.

Look at icons such as Abraham Lincoln, Oprah Whinfrey and Ervin "Magic" Johnson. Each one of them could have let their circumstances dictate who they were or what they would become. Instead of allowing their conditions and experiences to control them, they took steps to embrace the situation and were successful. They now have a passion to help, educate and support others on their own personal journey. What may have once been a "curse" was redefined as a "blessing" through a shifting of the mind, whether by President Lincoln, Oprah or Magic themselves or that of the community. *Note: This example is not to say to forget where you've been but to take note of your experiences, learn and grow from them and then allow yourself to determine where they will lead you.*

I remember speaking to a colleague of mine who chose to complete her Master's degree despite all odds against her. She had a significant impact on my life. As a teen parent, with no family support, she was determined to go to college. Although her extended family was not supportive, she was able to utilize her resources of friends to assist her with childcare and transportation as she worked and went to school. Technically, she could have been labeled a "statistic," according to society's standards, but her willpower and determination were strong enough that she knew giving up was not an option. She didn't want her son to be placed in foster care. Her dream was to go to college and make a difference in the world. She did not allow her circumstances to negatively determine the outcome of her future.

When we were children, it was different; the sky was the limit. We could be anyone we wanted to be, do anything we wanted to do, and no one would tell us differently. From Tinkerbell to a Policeman our imaginations would run rampid as our occupations and goals changed daily and no one questioned it. As teenagers, the American Dream was living in that big house on the hill with a white picket fence, two to three kids, and a dog. Anything was possible and within reach if we just believed. Nowadays, even our children don't have the same vision, imagination and belief we once had. What happened to society and our aspirations?

In a session with a young teen we were discussing her angry outbursts, use of strong language, and truancy at school. After several sessions it was determined that her dream was to be a Defense Attorney for children. It wasn't that she didn't have the ability, she had many of the needed skills at her fingertips, it was that she needed someone to take the time to believe and redirect her; providing guidance, mentorship and additional services to see her dream to fruition. She loved school – when she attended she did well and loved projects that she could research.

She was resourceful – she knew how to get around when she needed to. She was outspoken – she was able to tell people how she felt. She was an advocate – she was able to pinpoint the exact day and time someone did something to her enabling her to justify her escalating behavior. Who gives anyone the right to tell her who she will become? The ultimate result will be determined by the choices she makes throughout the rest of her life.

To start your journey on rekindling the inner you it is important to dream build – make a dreams list. Think back when you were that child or teenager. What did you wish for? As you got into your twenties, thirties and forties and so on... What was on your wish list that you couldn't do, have or experience because of other responsibilities or obligations? Don't base your answers on what others have told you or what you heard but on what you truly believe, feel and want.

Summary of Reflections:
Chapter 1 - Analysis

- Concentrate on the positive things in your life;
  Personal Note:

  _____

  _____

  _____

  _____

  _____

- Review your dreams daily;
  Personal Note:

  _____

  _____

  _____

  _____

  _____

- Take action over the things you have control over;
  Personal Note:

  _____

  _____

  _____

  _____

  _____

- Change the word "problem" to "challenge" in your vocabulary;

  Personal Note:

  _____

  _____

  _____

  _____

  _____

- Make a conscious decision to remove negative influences from your life;

  Personal Note:

  _____

  _____

  _____

  _____

  _____

- Go through the process and understand what you're doing is just as important as the end result;

  Personal Note:

  _____

  _____

  _____

  _____

  _____

- Believe in yourself and allow others to believe in you;

  Personal Note:

  _____

  _____

  _____

  _____

  _____

- Become conscious of the choices you make as they will impact your future.

  Personal Note:

  _____

  _____

  _____

  _____

  _____

Action Item Boot Camp:
Chapter 1 - Analysis

Exercise: Write down as many dreams as you can

With no limitations and the sky being the limit, finish the sentence.

If I could…

1. Do anything, I would…

_____

_____

_____

_____

_____

2. Go anywhere, I would…

_____

_____

_____

_____

_____

3. Have anything, I would…

_____

_____

_____

_____

_____

4. Be anything, I would…

_____

_____

_____

_____

_____

CHAPTER 2

The "Why" Factor

"Our business in life is not to get ahead of others but to get ahead of ourselves – to break our own records, to outstrip our yesterdays by our today; to do the little parts of our work with more force than ever before."
– Stewart Johnson

In the previous Chapter, we spoke about the importance of a dreams list. But, to actively see your dreams list come to fruition you need to know your "Why" Factor.

One day I asked myself what kept me going despite all the challenges I encountered. I had to identify what kept me going. How did I survive the battlefield of this thing I called life and all the drama it encompassed – bad and good. Drama doesn't always need to be distinguished as bad – you have the choice to redefine it for yourself.

For me it continues to be the joy of meeting new people, helping others and making a difference in their daily lives. Whether I'm providing therapy, coaching, mentoring or training, I find passion and purpose in helping others see their potential, conquer their dreams, overturn obstacles and achieve success. Ultimately, for me, it's important to "give back" to others. It's also the idea of spending quality time with family and those closest to me. It's the thought of not having to punch a time clock each morning but to sleep in without having that darn buzzer go off only to push that snooze button just one more time.

Identify your primary motivating factor. Look for that thing that keeps you fired up or energized; that gives you drive and purpose each and every day; then you will discover the ultimate driving force behind accomplishing your dreams.

Allan Pease, author of *Questions and Answers* said, "The most successful entrepreneurs in the world are driven by a cause, a reason, or a lifelong passion." What is it for you? Below are the nine motivating factors he has identified:

- Extra income
- More spare time
- Meeting new people
- Personal development
- Financial freedom
- Retirement
- Have own business
- Helping others
- Leaving a legacy

Everyone on this earth has a purpose although it may have yet to be defined. Others may be defined but are subject to change without notice due to circumstances and life situations. Spend some time defining your purpose. Go back to the basics of who you are, your foundation – Ground Zero, and discover what your purpose is or what you would like it to be. There is no absolute right or wrong answer so feel free to brainstorm.

For each agency, organization and program I've worked with, worked for, or founded, regardless of my position or title, I've made a commitment to leave a legacy. No matter how big or small, from executive management positions to my work as a volunteer, my purpose is to help those who cannot help themselves and give them a voice. My personal motivation encompasses every one of the key factors that Allan Pease speaks of during ones lifetime. I will touch on a few throughout this book.

The passion that you find in your daily work, work with others or by yourself is part of this equation. This could be that lifelong passion of yours – hobbies or interests. This may be your "Why" Factor. Think about the following:

- What do you enjoy doing during your spare time, who do you enjoy these activities with, if anyone, and why?

- When you are alone, what do you spend the most time doing that you enjoy and how does it make you feel?
- If you had more spare time or more money, what would you do and why?

Part of recognizing and identifying your passion is researching where the interest stems from. Who introduced it to you and what was the surrounding situation?

Look back at your dream analysis in the previous chapter and determine why those dreams are important to you. What is your "Why" Factor?

Summary of Reflections:
Chapter 2 - The "Why" Factor

- You are the Producer, Director, Writer, and Actor/Actress of your own drama which means because you set the stage, you can change the scenery, cast and storyline at any time. How the story not only develops but ends is totally up to you;
  Personal Note:

  _____

  _____

  _____

  _____

  _____

- Allow your experiences (good and bad) to be a stepping stone to your future;
  Personal Note:

  _____

  _____

  _____

  _____

  _____

- Identifying your Why Factor is the driving force behind you accomplishing your dreams;

  Personal Note:

  _____

  _____

  _____

  _____

  _____

- The most successful entrepreneurs are driven by a cause, reason or lifelong passion;

  Personal Note:

  _____

  _____

  _____

  _____

  _____

- Everyone has a purpose although it may have yet to be defined.

  Personal Note:

  _____

  _____

  _____

  _____

  _____

Action Item Boot Camp:
Chapter 2 - The "Why" Factor

Exercise: Take some time to brainstorm your Why factor. *(Use additional sheets if necessary)*

Ask yourself these things:

1. **Why are the dreams from the previous exercise important to you?**

   _____

   _____

   _____

   _____

   _____

2. **What motivates and drives you to wake up each and every morning?**

   _____

   _____

   _____

   _____

   _____

3. What are you passionate about?

_____

_____

_____

_____

_____

4. What will it enable you to do?

_____

_____

_____

_____

_____

5. How will it make you feel?

_____

_____

_____

_____

_____

Identifying Strengths

"What we see depends mainly on what we look for."
– John Lubbock

One of the most challenging things in life for some people is giving themselves kudos and identifying their personal strengths because to talk about your accomplishments or yourself is generally looked upon as being cocky, arrogant or conceited. I like to use the words, self-assured, proud and confident. Rarely do you hear others tell someone "You did a good job," "I love your smile," or "You are so down to earth." Why, because people, customarily, don't consciously practice giving others acknowledgements publicly. Rather, they keep it to themselves versus sharing those positive thoughts with others.

Today, companies have started recognizing that employee satisfaction is crucial in maintaining a productive environment and as a result they have begun restructuring policies and employee benefits offering promotions, accolades, and team building workshops to demonstrate staff appreciation. Although this is a nice beginning, what's missing is the ingredient to give their employees that cutting edge tool to use both inside and outside of the work arena. When I have my *Team Building: Universal Connection Workshops*, three topics I make sure to focus on are relationships, roles, communication and accountability; all of which can be fine tuned and improved upon in your personal or professional life .

With today's rigorous schedules, people often do not feel appreciated and supported which in turn, many times, results in dissatisfaction and unnecessary burnout, fatigue, depression, and feelings of worthlessness. This feeling can also be transferred into every aspect of your life, if not identified and controlled to the point where it eats at the very core of your energy. If this happens, it frequently limits your ability to stay focused while juggling and flipping schedules to appease others. To assist with identifying your strengths in the midst of life's challenges, let's look at what I call the Circle of Strength.

The Circle of Strength is broken up into 3 Core Areas all of which intermingle, interchangeably while celebrating personal uniqueness:

- Accomplishments
- Physical Traits
- Personality Characteristics

Accomplishments

Accomplishment is a broad term and is defined in *Webster's Dictionary* as: 1. Completion 2. Work completed. 3. A social art or skill. Within this definition is a range of idioms that can be used to describe how one personally defines ones accomplishments. I like to think of it in general terms as "things you are most proud of."

To take ownership of my life, I first must acknowledge that I have a "busy" schedule, an "active" lifestyle, and understand if I don't choose to change it, I must accept it. *Note: I didn't say I had to like it.* Let's be honest, regardless of whether we're talking about me or you, the choice is still ours and ours alone on whatever we decide to do with our lives, but if we choose to accept it as is, we also must accept all the unmentionables that go along with it – both positive and negative. We change the things we can and work through the things we cannot. The reason why I say work through is that whether we like it or not, we will always go through something less desiring and it's better to learn how to work through it to gain momentum and control over our feelings and emotions attached to the situation, before the situation has more power and takes control over us.

I remember when I had a big decision whether I was going to allow my oldest daughter to go away for school versus attend the local high school. I was fully aware of the sacrifices everyone would need to make and I also knew the biggest strain would be the commute. And, yes, I received a lot of discouragement but I also received positive support. Ultimately, I knew it was a decision my family and I would have to make together since it impacted everyone, yet in order for them to buy into the idea, I knew I had to research, do my homework and develop a concrete plan that would work for the entire family. This is where I used my *Vida Blueprint of Success (VBS) System*.

I was able to utilize my "Worksheet Analyzer" to come up with the possible solutions to every potential obstacle I might encounter, identifying my strengths and limitations and actively visualizing the plan before I discussed it with the family and put it in motion. Then I used my "System Coordinator" to plug in my feelings from the "Analyzer," attaching benchmarks to put the plan into motion, incorporating each aspect of my life. I reviewed my "Financial Organizer" to verify any potential hardships that may incur with this transition and lastly the "Benchmark Recorder" to process and evaluate the journey of my plan's success.

The situation definitely wasn't easy but by using the VBS System, I regained belief in not only myself and my abilities but identified new strengths in each and every family member and our family is stronger for it.

Ask the question: Who Am I? Who Am I includes your physical traits, personality characteristics, proud moments and what sets you apart from others – your uniqueness. If you've ever had the opportunity to attend one of my Steppin' 2 the Future (S2F) events, you would've seen the youth I work with do their Who Am I insignia. This is one of the things we're known for. For more information on Steppin' 2 The Future, visit: http://www.steppin2thefuture.org.

Who you are from past to present will impact who you can and will become in the future – a survivor. This is one thing we all have in common. Make a conscious decision and accept the responsibility that this is part of who you are. Once again, the word "survivor" is a term only and does not have to be defined as negative. If this is what you're currently thinking, go back and shift your mindset by reviewing what you learned in Chapter 1 - Analysis. We have all survived something – struggles, disappointments, loss, and/or hardships, but we've all made it through and will continue to do so. No matter how you look at it, we've independently survived that less than perfect situation or crisis and therefore it is termed a strength. It doesn't matter if it didn't turn out exactly how you wanted it, you survived it and that's something to celebrate.

Graduating from school (regardless of whether it was kindergarten, graduate school or somewhere in between) was something worth celebrating as was having children and getting married. In addition, I have had smaller not so recognizable celebrations as well such as getting out of bed when I was tired, going to work when I was sick and helping others when it was inconvenient. Regardless of when these experiences and situations occurred, they will always be fundamental in who I am and who I have become.

So, as you can see, anything can be identified as a strength from the biggest of accomplishments to the smallest gestures. It's important to acknowledge everything and celebrate them as they occur because every accomplishment is the driving force to a more recognizable, achievable you.

For example, take a person who was once happily married and then found themselves divorced. The experience of happily married to divorce is still a recognizable aspect of who that person is based on their personal journey and how they processed the information. The divorce was the event however the underlying emotions, reactions and overall experience to that specified event will change a portion of who that person is. It doesn't need to be a big or small impact, positive or negative, but the realization is that the person will be affected and the character of the person will be improved.

Each person's character is unique and what may greatly impact one person may have a very different affect on someone else. So for this particular set of divorced individuals, it is recommended that they celebrate the good times, celebrate what they learned from the not so pleasant moments and then celebrate their ability to accept the situation and/or move forward with their own individuality and independence.

This is what I term *flip the script*. You take something bad or negative and then flip and redefine it to a more powerful, optimistic outcome. *Take note: the script is the event or situation that occurred that you would like to change in some way, shape or form.* Being able to master *flip the script* takes practice and skill, and when done correctly, is a strength. You can turn any negative situation into something positive if you learn how to flip the situation correctly. Don't ever discount your past (good or bad) as it is a stepping stone to your future.

This is the difference between having a bad day or a character building day. I learned the phrase "character building day" from Motivational Speaker, Willie Jolley and have used it time and time again in moments where all I could do was exhale. When my day has been less then desirable, and people ask me how I'm doing, I don't claim the negativity and tell them I had a bad day. This would only result in an ongoing conversation of describing what happened, adding fuel to the fire and the not so glamorous emotions attached to the days experiences leaving me worn out and dismissed. No, I tell them with a smile – I had a character building day which somehow releases all the inhibitions and stresses I had no control over thereby taking ownership and not buying into the negativity.

When reviewing your character building day, ask yourself: what did you learn? Does your attitude need an adjustment? Does a mind shift need to be made?

The quality of people you hang around or associate with can have a long lasting affect on your life and may reduce your lifespan if negative. Do you have the strength and confidence to live your legacy and increase your self esteem? Remember, your input determines your output. What you choose to believe, listen to and watch will have an affect on your overall being.

Example:

- What do you listen to in the car – loud music or inspirational cd's;
- What do you read;
- What do you watch on television;
- If someone cuts you off while driving or talking, how do you react?
- Do you associate with positive or negative people?

Here's an example using *Flip the Script*:

Real Situation: I left late for an appointment and then hit traffic which delayed me even further.

Flip the Script: If I would've left on time, I could've potentially been involved in the multi-car accident I passed on the freeway.

For every negative outcome, you should come up with a positive reward that's tangible. I realized I could have been involved, but I wasn't. After reviewing my daily routine on the freeway I was aware that this particular day was different. Around the time the accident occurred I knew, by repetition, that usually I would've been passing that particular area, in that particular lane, when the accident occurred, as it was my daily routine. I owned it enabling me to flip the script, deescalating my tension and stress to keep me level headed until I reached my destination.

Your ability to flip the script is your own private, personal process. You don't need anyone to buy into your view, understand it nor do you need their approval.

Physical Traits

Physically, what is one trait you like about yourself (eg. eyes, smile, dimples, etc…). Usually, identifying one trait is somewhat easy but identifying more than one tends to be more of a challenge because it's easier to point out what physically needs improving (eg. weight, hair, stomach, etc…). Remember what I said previously, we are our own worse critics and that is a habit that is hard to break but let's once again flip the script. Although you may not like your *blank*, it is important to determine what sets you apart from others making you unique and different.

Just the fact that there's only one De Vida Bell, with my background, my experiences and my thoughts makes me different and unique. Even if I was a twin, and our experiences were the same, our views and emotions to a particular situation may be different.

We all have "special" qualities. It may be your dimples, long legs or love handles that make you unique and different. It's not so important what others think of your physical traits but how you think and feel within yourself. If you need help, feel free to consider the view of those you respect and trust. If you feel comfortable, ask what specifically they like about the physical trait they've identified. If they're truly someone you can confide in, they'll be open to explaining their opinion. Formulate your own opinion and either add it to your strengths list – a new self discovery - or discard it.

Personality Characteristics

Identifying Personality Characteristics is the last core area on the Circle of Strength. Character is the internal part of you – incorporating your personality, belief system and how you carry and see yourself. I may see myself as assertive, but others may see it as aggressive. The same is true for self confidence versus conceit.

I believe I am a creative, energetic person who sees strengths and qualities in others that they don't necessarily see in themselves. These are some of my strengths. When people introduce themselves, they customarily use statements indicating their degree, title in an agency or an organization versus their first and last name only allowing others to make their own decision regarding their internal classification.

For example, you could be the CEO of a major cooperation but be unethical and have a less than desirable personality. On the other hand, a person with the same status could be open minded and be able to work under dire circumstances while working outside the box and encouraging others to do the same. A person's degree or title is not what is important but how the person leads.

Please understand status and money does not make an individual. It is who you are internally and what you present to the world that identifies and defines you.

Summary of Reflections:
Chapter 3 - Identifying Strengths

- Acknowledge the type of lifestyle you have and make changes as needed to accommodate the lifestyle you want;

  Personal Note:

  _____

  _____

  _____

  _____

  _____

- Accept responsibility for the lifestyle you choose – choose to control your lifestyle versus your lifestyle controlling you;

  Personal Note:

  _____

  _____

  _____

  _____

  _____

- Accept who you are as a person;
  Personal Note:

  _____

  _____

  _____

  _____

  _____

- Change the things you can, and work through the things you can't;
  Personal Note:

  _____

  _____

  _____

  _____

  _____

- Anything can be identified as a strength. Celebrate all of your accomplishments – big and small;
  Personal Note:

  _____

  _____

  _____

  _____

  _____

- When you feel distressed, flip the script and determine something positive that happened from the situation;

  Personal Note:

  _____

  _____

  _____

  _____

  _____

- Don't shun or discount your past (good/bad) as it is a stepping stone to your future;

  Personal Note:

  _____

  _____

  _____

  _____

  _____

- Being unique and different is a strength;

  Personal Note:

  _____

  _____

  _____

  _____

  _____

- It's not as important what others think of you but what you think of yourself;

  Personal Note:

  _____

  _____

  _____

  _____

  _____

- Understand status and money doesn't make the individual; it's who you are as a person and what you present to the world that identifies you.

  Personal Note:

  _____

  _____

  _____

  _____

  _____

Action Item Boot Camp:
Chapter 3 - Identifying Strengths

In this exercise, stretch yourself to list **at least three things for each item**. The more you list, the more you can embark on your own self-discovery:

1. **List the qualities you have that have enabled you to juggle your "busy" schedule and/or live your "active" lifestyle**

    _____

    _____

    _____

    _____

    _____

2. **List the qualities about yourself that have helped you get through the challenging times in your life**

    _____

    _____

    _____

    _____

    _____

3. List the accomplishments you are most proud of

_____

_____

_____

_____

_____

4. List some situations where you have impacted someone else's life in a positive way

_____

_____

_____

_____

_____

5. List what you physically like about yourself

_____

_____

_____

_____

_____

6. **If you were writing to a pen pal, describe to that person who you are by listing some of your personality characteristics**

_____

_____

_____

_____

_____

Goals

"A goal without a plan is just a wish."
– Antoine de Saint-Exupery

In Chapter 2, we talked about finding your "Why" Factor. The very thing that gets you pumped up and motivated to exceed your wildest dreams. In that, you identified your passion but there's a big difference between passion, goals and dreams.

Passion keeps you interested and excited to achieve your goals.

Goals keep you focused and give you benchmarks to achieve your accomplishments and dreams.

Dreams give you energy and motivation. Fulfilled dreams are the foundation from which your legacy is derived.

When you define your dreams in detail, you actively visualize what it looks like laying the foundation of your goals. Goals should be defined in categories (example: emotional well-being) as they are the stepping stones to fulfilling your dreams in every aspect of your life.

Within each of these stepping stones are incrementally designated tasks or strategies that you employ to reach that independent goal.

For example, if I have a goal to loose weight, I may place this goal in my physical well-being category and one of my tasks or action items may be to find a personal trainer within a twenty mile radius of my home and make a commitment to losing weight. Notice I said *will* versus *can*. The word *will* puts an accountability factor on the task whereas the word *can* leaves things open for negotiation and the "but" factor. I know I should go to the gym today "but" my soap is on tv. I know I should do my sit-ups "but" I had a long day at work and I am too tired.

With each goal, designate a timeframe for each task to be completed and write it down. Writing down your goal, with a due date, puts an urgency on the task. I heard it said that ideas are not goals until you put a deadline on it.

Goals are derived from an overall purpose. Using the weight loss goal example above, let's identify the purpose of why someone may want to loose weight.

- Twenty year reunion
- Physical health
- Too fit into a particular outfit

These particular reasons may be the "why" factor for loosing the weight. It's the reason behind the goal, behind the action.

When I decided to write this book my goal was to give other people with busy schedules and active lifestyles a simple guide to motivate and recharge themselves in easy to follow steps so that they could continue multitasking in the midst of life's daily challenges and transitions. My deadline for this book was my 40th birthday. My "why" factor was to help others, like myself, work through the daily grind of life while moving forward in a positive direction.

I knew from experience what is was like to have negativity surround me when I was trying to stay positive, putting an added strain on my energy causing fatigue, burnout and not feeling appreciated in different aspects of my life. I knew something had to change – not only the people I surrounded myself with, from personal to professional, but also my own expectations and how I treated myself. I began to redevelop, relearn and redefine what I learned and experienced since childhood to the current day, from personal values to professional ethics, redesigning and creating tools to help me be a survivor of life's challenges.

Today, I have a renewed sense of purpose and I'm energized with a new set of expectations not only for myself but those I associate with. And yes, my active lifestyle still remains but I'm blessed to be able to have the energy and passion to look beyond the walls of traditional methods to create new resources and opportunities to reach my desired goals that work for me with my forever changing schedule. I wanted to be able to share with others the tools I learned, created and developed, that worked for me so that they too may not falter at the hands of others or themselves enabling them to recharge during their most dire of circumstances and challenging times.

Everyone can benefit from a positive stroke as well as emotional support but expecting to receive it solely from others has the potential to lead to disappointment and heartbreak. So, instead we empower ourselves to give it to ourselves by treating ourselves with respect, dignity, self-praises, mini celebrations and rewards. No one can justify who you are, how you should feel, or make you feel bad without your permission.

Goals are a vital part of charging forward to uncover not only your hidden talents but can manifest themselves into helping you achieve accomplishments leading to success.

Summary of Reflections:
Chapter 4 - Goals

- Passion keeps you interested and excited and gives you a desire to achieve your goals;
  Personal Note:

  _____

  _____

  _____

  _____

  _____

- Goals keep you focused toward your dream;
  Personal Note:

  _____

  _____

  _____

  _____

  _____

- Dreams give you energy and motivation;
  Personal Note:

  _____

  _____

  _____

  _____

  _____

- Defining your dreams in detail lays the foundation for your goals;

  Personal Note:

  _____

  _____

  _____

  _____

  _____

- Defining dreams in categories connects you to fulfilling dreams in every aspect of your life;

  Personal Note:

  _____

  _____

  _____

  _____

  _____

- Decide on a deadline for each goal and write it down;

  Personal Note:

  _____

  _____

  _____

  _____

  _____

- Treat yourself with respect, dignity, self-praises, and mini celebrations and rewards;
  Personal Note:

  _____

  _____

  _____

  _____

  _____

- No one can justify who you are, how you should feel, or make you feel badly without your permission.
  Personal Note:

  _____

  _____

  _____

  _____

  _____

Action Item Boot Camp:
Chapter 4 - Goals

Think about the details of each of your goals as you complete each exercise below:

1. **List your top three current goals and categorize them**

   _____

   _____

   _____

   _____

   _____

2. **Visually think about each of those goals and write the details for each below** *(use a separate sheet of paper if necessary)*

   _____

   _____

   _____

   _____

   _____

3.

4. **Brainstorm strategies or action items to reach each desired goal**

   _____

   _____

   _____

   _____

   _____

5. **Assign a deadline to each action item and goal**

   _____

   _____

   _____

   _____

   _____

6. **List some ways you can praise yourself**

   _____

   _____

   _____

   _____

   _____

7. **Of the three goals listed earlier, indicate three ways you can celebrate or reward yourself**

   _____

   _____

   _____

   _____

   _____

CHAPTER 5

Legacy

"Doing what you love is the cornerstone of having
abundance in your life."
– Dr. Wayne Dyer

Legacy is divided into three main areas of your life:

- Personal Life
- Professional Life
- Community Life

To define your legacy starts with writing your personal "living" eulogy. Yes, I said eulogy. Thinking negative thoughts or morbidity? – It's time to do a mind shift (See Chapter 1). This eulogy is a living, breathing document, similar to that of a living will, which can be edited at any given moment. It is a personal depiction of how you want to have lived your life, be remembered or would want others to say about you in your absence. It is documented in journal format with a beginning, middle and end.

Think about it as though you were writing a play or story of your life with everything accessible at your fingertips.

Although you are the star, you choose the other characters, the roles (villains and heroes), as well as decide the who, what, where, when and how each person comes into and affects each aspect of your life. You set the stage, scenery, drama and format. You have the discretion to change the characters and roles as needed to get the end result. The end result is the storyline or plot for how you want others to remember you. In addition to the Lead Role, you are the Creator, Director, Producer, Writer and Editor, etc. The story is not built in concrete and is subject to change without notice.

By developing this living document on paper, and reviewing it daily, you unconsciously claim ownership of your desired lifestyle by mixing and matching circumstances, setting goals, creating strategies and setting deadlines for the preferred outcomes. Doing this will enable you to put your actions into motion. As your lifestyle changes, you should set in motion the life you want to lead. If you want success, define what success means to you and then associate with like minded people. The same is true for any other strengths you want to develop or goals you want to reach; associate with others to support and partner with you in your journey.

When people say they are successful, what does that really mean? Success means different things to different people. Some associate success with money, whether it's how much you have, how much you make or how much you've saved. Others will associate success with materialistic items and possessions. And the third definition is associated with internal values – what people are able to unconditionally give and share with others; the love, union and fellowship of family and friends.

I remember hearing about a time when my girls were out with my mother on an educational excursion at a jewelry store differentiating the clarity and origin of different kinds of pearls and stones. They wanted to understand why their (costume) jewelry looked different than that of grown-ups. My youngest daughter at the time was six or seven and stated to my mother, in an excited voice:

"Grandmommy, you're rich," as she closely examined her string of pearls.

My mother responded with a beaming smile, "Yes, I'm rich because I have grandchildren."

It's extraordinary to listen to the defining views of what success is from children to adults as well as peer to peer. But what's also interesting is those same definitions can get so easily misinterpreted. There is another term called luck that many times gets confused with the word success or is sometimes used interchangeably.

Success is reaching any goal you may have for yourself – big or small.

Luck is when preparation meets opportunity.

Both of these terms are subject to interpretation. One could also challenge that both luck and success can be equally defined as a person being in the right place at the right time. What happens when luck and success come together? You add it as another chapter in your living eulogy, the building blocks of the legacy you will leave behind.

Part of developing your legacy, writing your story or recording your living eulogy is reflecting on the dreams and goals throughout your life. Need help, return to Chapter 3 on Identifying Strengths and review your personal notes in the Summary of Reflections section and exercises in the Action Item Boot Camp. Remember, dreams give you energy and goals keep you focused. I encourage you to review your dreams list in Chapter 1 as well.

Within the three areas of Legacy: Personal Life, Professional Life, and Community Life, it's infrequent that the three entities can be in unison. How you might be remembered in your personal life may be completely different than that of your professional or community life. The perfect balance would be to have a summation of you as a person where everyone has the same "positive" things to say about you. Few people have the ultimate universal balance within their lives.

Although some of us strive for perfection others may be great with their family but lousy colleagues or are workaholics with no time to spend with family or friends. The same is true for those who donate generously to charities but are penny-pinching with their family. Somehow or other, there's a missing link and the more we can strive for that 1% improvement in every area within ourselves, the more our own imperfections will slowly be shifted into incremental accomplishments.

Summary of Reflections:
Chapter 5 - Legacy

- A living eulogy is a living document of how you want to have lived your life, be remembered and want others to say about you in your absence;

  Personal Note:

  _____

  _____

  _____

  _____

  _____

- Review your living eulogy daily to unconsciously claim ownership to that desired lifestyle, set your goals, create strategies and put a deadline on the preferred outcome;

  Personal Note:

  _____

  _____

  _____

  _____

  _____

- Define your goals and what success means to you and then associate with like minded people;

  Personal Note:

  _____

  _____

  _____

  _____

  _____

- Success is reaching any goal you may have for yourself – big or small; Luck is when preparation meets opportunity;

  Personal Note:

  _____

  _____

  _____

  _____

  _____

Action Item Boot Camp:
Chapter 5 - Legacy

Think about what you would write in your "living" eulogy:

1. **What would you like to be remembered for**

    _____

    _____

    _____

    _____

    _____

2. **What would you like others to say about you**

    _____

    _____

    _____

    _____

    _____

3. **What gift would you like to leave that others would remember you by**

    _____

    _____

    _____

    _____

    _____

4. How have you made a difference or impacted someone's life

   _____

   _____

   _____

   _____

   _____

5. Define what success means to you

   _____

   _____

   _____

   _____

   _____

6. How are you going to prepare for luck should it happen? What preparations do you need to make should the opportunity you've been waiting for present itself

   _____

   _____

   _____

   _____

   _____

7. **What is the legacy you want to leave in your personal life, professional life and community life.**
   (Use additional sheets if needed)

   _____

   _____

   _____

   _____

   _____

CHAPTER 6

Simplicity

"Often people attempt to live their lives backwards: they try to have more things, or more money, in order to do more of what they want so they will be happier. The way it actually works is the reverse. You must first be who you really are, then do what you live to do, in order to have what you want." – Margaret Young

Throughout this Book, I guided you on a journey to eliminate the burnout and rekindle the passion within. I've provided detailed concepts and tools for you to use as you take the next three steps to rejuvenate the inner you. Reviewing your personal notes at the end of each chapter and boot camp exercises regularly will assist and prepare you to control life's transitions and circumstances shifting any negativity or downward spiral you may encounter. By reviewing and mastering the tools, set forth in previous chapters, you will be able to recharge yourself and take action to live a more fruitful and positive YOU.

Step 1: Who Am I

Getting back to basics should be simpler to do, now that you've learned "The How." Identify your strengths, rekindle your dreams and find your passion. Continue to document as you discover new things about yourself and give yourself kudos. Add to your dreams list whenever possible, detailing every aspect through active visualization and keep it growing, setting goals and deadlines, checking off your accomplishments and celebrating each one independently.

Step 2: Redirect Your Attitude

Remember negativity breeds negativity. Make that mind shift switch whenever you need to diffuse negativity and embrace positivity. Review your dreams and goals and take action benchmarking deadlines to your ideas. Don't lay idle and expect positive results. Capture your vision and allow it to take you to where you want to go. Connect with like minded people and make each life's action a component to you reaching your goals, dreams or legacy.

Step 3: Invest In Yourself

Be consciously aware of what you are reading, listening to and with whom you associate. Jot down your favorite personal affirmations and inspirational quotes and review them daily. Read thirty minutes daily, minimally, to stimulate your mind and keep it soaring to new heights of self-discovery. Challenge yourself to research and read things you wouldn't normally such as biographies, autobiographies, a different hobby (i.e. cooking, photography) and see if it sparks some interest. Attend personal or professional development seminars, find a personal life coach and treat yourself to that weekend massage, golf tournament, island resort, private dinner, book or movie.

Remember, YOU define what success means to you. YOU determine the choices you make, and YOU create the lifestyle you seek.

*"You don't get in life what you ask for;
you get in life what you go for."*
– David Bach

ABOUT THE AUTHOR

De Vida Bell is no stranger to a "busy" schedule. As a mother and a wife of an "active" household, her lifestyle is nothing but extraordinary. She had to learn how to juggle, be flexible and set priorities while maintaining a sense of peace and connection within herself. Although it wasn't always easy, she learned through trial and error and by a process of elimination how to reduce her unwarranted stressors and find her "me" time while balancing everyone's extracurricular activities and appointments without sacrificing her family's needs or substituting her education or job commitments.

For years De Vida educated professionals and students how to reach their full potential, personally and professionally, by offering trainings and workshops to individuals and businesses alike. As a Licensed Clinical Social Worker and an alumnus of the University of Southern California, School of Social Work, her life has been dedicated to training professionals on lifestyle balance, working with "at-risk," underserved youth and youth leaders as well as aspiring entrepreneurs, entertainers, and service professionals. She continues to work as a therapist, mentor, consultant, speaker, advocate and coach.

De Vida has made several guest appearances speaking at high schools, performing arts studios, community organizations, programs and county facilities including: The Department of: Probation, Mental Health, and Children and Family Services. In 2004 she developed the ALI Curriculum and founded Steppin' 2 The Future (S2F), a 501c (3) non-profit organization dedicated to youth, education, leadership and the arts. In 2005 she created the Vida Blueprint of Success (VBS) System, through her company Mahogany Vida Enterprises, incorporating both structure and flexibility in all the many facets of a person's life enabling them to balance and provide a sense of accomplishment personally and professionally.

Notes

Notes